2E: EDUCATION AND ECONOMY

OPEN LEARNING, ETHICAL CAPITALISM

MOHAMMAD YOUNUS

Contents

Preface

Author's word

Repetition and grammatical errors are conscious decision, if found. Do not consider it error and repetition is unnecessary, it is the format or method of writing. There is no room for question of format and linguistic issues, these are theories and concepts presenting or expressing in certain way. The ideas and views can be caught, the thoughts and wisdom can be found.

Thank You.

Younus.words@gmail.com

Index

CHAPTER I

OPEN EDUCATION

INTRODUCTION

*'I cannot teach anybody anything, I can only make them think' – **Socrates**.*

*'If you can't explain it simply, you don't understand it well enough'- **Albert Einstein**.*

Human beings are naturally learned i.e. not ignorant. [Human beings may have illiteracy, illiteracy is not ignorance.] Education is the transmission or description or analysis of world's status before human beings so that human beings can smartly act or react to it. Education is the founding pillars of the world and human civilization in different forms, it could build better world. Human lead the world, education serves the human. Education is a human trust, it empowers human being. Education is fundamental and recognized global culture and custom of today, human beings are practiced or performed it religiously and submit his golden hours of life before education with all the resources. Education builds an individuality of human beings, make them free or independent.

Education is individualized concept, it only works for individual or human reason. It does not have any control over its impacts or influences, neither it decided to create any impact or influences over anything. It delivers and describes or analyzes the issues to support human reason only, individual decide the matter using his own reasoning which may be good or bad in different perspective but education does not decide or define it. Education is absolutely targeted to individual human reason, to serve

1

and support individual human reason is all about education. Neither it decides about good or bad reasoning nor targeted to make any impacts or influences on anything else. Cuckoos are singing soulfully in his own mind, someone get disturbed and someone get enjoyed but cuckoos does not have any interest in making anyone happy or unhappy as it sing as it his religion. Education is service, it does not set the things. Its job only to serve for individual human reason, not define or decide on anything includes human reason.

Education is messenger only, it does not have own independent target or goals. Education does not set to make any results, it does not decide. It may be wished to be citizen individual and independent but it cannot be followed it in framing its curriculum. The content it deliver has own intrinsic purpose but the only job of the education is to good delivery of messages without any distortion or manipulation as messenger and nothing more, rest is on individual to decide or work upon it. Education do not want to do anything, education do not want to make anyone anything, it is not the education. Education support to think, it gives all the description and analysis in an easy or understandable manner to think critically and decide. To support or nurture human reason is education, not create or change human reason. Human reason is the centre of education, education is the slave or servant of human reason only and the only job of the education is to serve the master i.e. human reason religiously. A slave does not have any own goal or freedom or wish, he submits completely before his master and slavery or service with full of devotion to the master is his life all about. Education is slave of human reason only, it does not produce slave for own or others.

Follow or support human instinct and human reason are education, to understand or explore human nature critically is one purpose of the education. A free and natural grown up environment to discover oneself, know thyself. Find human instinct and human reason in exploring, acceleration of human reason. The issues or world status articulate and describe in a systematic way to enhance or cultivate human reason, education is great description of things.

Education is searching something or seeking truth, understanding the world and individual instinct or passion. Searching the answer of many unanswered questions of the world, searching his inherent instinct or interests. Searching the road to get or accomplish his love, searching his identity and status. Searching something unknown but thirst for unknown, waiting for the day or events that connect and get enlightened. Searching something known but needs recognition or validation, searching something not getting anywhere, searching his soul. Searching answer and question, searching love and pain, searching identity and interest, searching the way to get and hope to connect, searching known and unknown, searching soul and dreams, searching the truth and false. Education is holding its curriculum and system, you are checking and searching yours own something here which may found or not. Education at his job, you are at your job and everything or everyone is at own job in this world. Education is one of the searching or seeking platform or tools, searching...

Education is not system to be copied in life, it is not religion to be devoted. It is way of learning, it delivers different learning materials. Education itself is not any dogma or idol, it is platform or environment of learning and study. There is nothing permanent to follow or copy or adopt, it does not owe any moral or ideal standard. There is no definition or face or color of 'educated' or uneducated, you may defined literate or illiterate. Education does not guarantee anything, it does not have any quantified absolute responsibility at all. Education describes or analyzes, not decide or create. Education does not have its own product, it sells or delivers others product through salesman or delivery boy. Education is not role model or personality or ideology, it does not have fix formal structure or standard or idea or model to define it or follow it. It is only a description or delivery system, it does not decide or create or manufacture anything. Take support or resource from education only if requires and decide or create own way or status or life. Education is not judge, it shall not pass any verdict.

Education does not have the principles of right or wrong, truth or false, good or bad, just or unjust, moral or immoral etc. Education does not decide, it describe only. Military education or spy education or sex education is also education which covers rape, murder, theft etc; in that sense there is no right or wrong education. There is quality education or not, there is efficient education or not, there is relevant education or not can make a point. There are no moral or ethical standard of education, it may has some practical or quality standard of education. Education taught morality or ethics without being moral or ethical.

Education is time pass in leisure or environment to grow up a child or waste of time, when human being does not have or unable to work to do then they go for education. Human beings can utilize or work only 15%-20% time of his life, they systematized or bound to waste 80% time of life. At child or adult age i.e. before 20 years old and at old age human beings are completely incapable to do any real work, then they waste huge amount of time in maintenance of themselves and in failure or experiencing. They got 10-20 years to work at young and capable age, among this time they waste a huge amount of time for maintenance and experiencing failure or waiting for something. Finally, he got 10%-15% time or 10 years highest to work and build something properly. More than 80% time of life is leisure or time pass only, people go for education at this leisure to time pass or waste of time who are either waiting for growing up or dying. Education is time pass in leisure or waste of time, if missed then the basic education like literacy is serious concern even at work.

Education is the methods of disseminating information and communicating or connecting with others. Education informs or presents the information or facts but it cannot decide or fix. Education tells stories of the ages, with the ages or context education stream or ways has been changed. Education follow the wind, it does not control or challenge the wind. The way makes it or the age stories gave it, education follow and act upon it. There is no fix or standard definition or way of education, it is flexible or follow the power or age. Once ethics or wisdom was education, today skill or excellence is the education. Once education was for civilization, today education is for high consumption. Once education was dignity, today education is commodity. Once education was religion, today education is science. Education does not choose its path, time has chosen the path for education.

It is a million dollar question of today that whether education should have basic or fundamental structure? Whether education should be commoditize or privatize or capitalize or materialize? Can education be an independent entity or institution? Whether education shall be secular, separates or free from political and religious undue influences? Whether education is training for slavery or license to forced brainwash for serving others agenda or interests? Right to right education shall be ensured, curriculum shall be unbiased and open or universalized. Education is the founding pillars of the modern civilization, today education is a human trust. Education is not propaganda machine, education shall not be waste of golden hours of youth. Education is inclusive but not exclusive, education is free or open to present all and rest up to free choice of learner. Education is ocean of resources which shall not be imposed censorship, allow others to swim and find. Education is not training for slavery but freedom of choice, education empowers but not enslave. When there was no education that time also human beings were fulfilling their material needs i.e. eating, sleeping, having sex etc. Education is not only employment but also enlightenment, education is not trading commodity but a dignified public service. Education has its inherent nature or fundamental principles, it shall be understood and respected for better education towards building a better nation or world.

Education does not guarantee happiness, education is led by the reason and happiness is choice made by the reason. Education gives you description and analysis of things, you have to make choice or decision or find what you want. Education tells you the way, you have to get it done. Education does not guarantee any results or it does not decide anything of your life, it is you to decide or make results where education may support and may not. Education does not have any standard, neither it does guarantee you happiness nor it does make you a better person. Education does not have any independent identity or religion, it gives you only update about status of the situation or circumstances and sometimes with analysis report which may be correct and maybe not. It's you to decide or make choice, to make it real you may take support from different tools where one may be education only. Do not overrate education, don't be delusive on education.

Education and social order are not connected, education cannot decide peoples interest or instinct or passion and cannot decide social order accordingly. Everyone has distinct natural interest, education may help you to think to make it better but education cannot change it. Human beings are naturally diversified or classified, education may deliver more resources to think critically to make things better like science& technology. Social order builds or breaks and decided by many other factors including natural factors, education helps the existing order to be better but not break or build.

Education revolutionizes or formalize through innovating writing, printing press and finally education technology. The nature of education is information and communication in a better or broader way, reading and writing. The availability, accessibility and affordability of information or knowledge are the inherent instinct of education. Education technology makes it reach to the highest peak of its goal, today 'learning' is more used term instead of 'education'.

To learn local and international or other different languages with four modules which are reading, writing, speaking and listening i.e. (formal or informal) communication or literacy is the basics of education. Language is the foundation to learn or acquire knowledge, great way to get education. Language has different important aspects includes social, cultural, political, psychological, global etc. and it provides authentic information which is real or true. The well understanding of language does not mere as way of acquiring knowledge but in a true way of analyzing the knowledge. Language is way of communication, connection, and coordination for better education and for better living. Everything has language, it is the access key. Who understands the language well, they understand the thing well.

Recording or documentation i.e. writing is the foundation of modern education, it helps to disseminate the information or knowledge vastly. Undoubtedly, invention of writing has played an important role in the human progress. Writing is human consciousness, there are different style or format of writing in own letters or characters. Where language has got its formal structure there writing invents. Alphabet and its formation has long history, it takes long and repeated practice or revisions to get recognized alphabetic structure of today in different language and writing. Writing is a human conscious process of expressing views, it documents and disseminates the information and knowledge. It delivers content for education, get high and easy accessibility for education. Not only documentation in pen and paper but also today keyboard and files are recording includes in different formats like video, audio, image, document etc. Documentation and dissemination of content is the key components of education, it makes the AVAILABILITY of knowledge which is the main purpose of education. Education is not forced manipulation or brainwashing machine but it makes the information and knowledge available only which freely choose by the learner, education describes only but not decides. There is no common standard or way to enforce for all, individual decides. Everyone has different potentials or inherent instinct or passion which is unchangeable but supportive, people will follow that ultimately and education may support or assist. Education empowered people, not overpowered.

Feelings convert into words or expression is complicated where human follow the ancient first, gradually it gets shape and structured or filtered common characters that recognized by mass people. It develops and describes the grammar structures to understand and learn language deeply. Language and its different format like speaking or writing is customary and capable to work, it connects people and recognized by the mass people. Everyone has language and own style or way or format, to connect and express of human thoughts one to another is the key purpose and standard of language. It does not have fix or pure and exact or permanent format or standard. It's dynamic, change and develops. Language is name or identity, it has huge impacts on human beings mentally and physically. Language has its own nature or expression or impression or character or soul and mode or presentation or appeal or spirit or rhythm. Language beauty and brain, it is meaningful love. Language is the foundation and basics or soul of the education with common purpose of both that connect and communicate, the more understanding of language you have the more you will learn deep.

Education was personalized and community based in ancient time, by the time education develops through innovation and integration. Human development is making education more important, education is contributing to human civilization materially and immaterially. Education is innovating and protecting human civilization, education became founding pillars of modern civilization. Education is local and global agenda today, education is the leader and sustainer of the modern civilization. Education is the global culture that binds and protects all, instruments to discover human potentials and its highest utilization.

Education for the protection or maintenance and development or progress of existing civilization, education does not create new civilization. It bears, own and protect or carry or take forward the civilization. Education is the witness of the civilization, it is not creator of the civilization. It follows and describes, it does not create or decide. The civilization create or has been born by human only, education may or may not be there. The system is creation or creature, it cannot create. Human beings are the creator, they shall not be in delusion of system will create. The systems follow the human, human lead the system. The dependency on the system to dictate human will end the world and no creation or new beginning. System is tools created by human to serve human things, system cannot lead or rule over human. Education shall serve the human civilization, it contributes in academia of human civilization that works to protect and progress of the human civilization. Education is the history, it analyze the past in the context of present but future will only decided by human who may be in the classroom or maybe not. It inspires or encourages or supports but innovation or revolution or renaissance ultimately shall led by the human actively. Education cannot create you but it can make you better. Education is the civil servant where human beings are the prime minister or president. Education implement and maintain the progress of human laws and policies, education is the loyal servant of human civilization.

Education superpower or global education centre or great education system i.e. education culture or education politics, educate the world and build or lead the future world the way you want. Economic development is important to be education superpower, education and economy both are interdependent. Education superpower is not only about better education system but better space (specialized towns of education), better environment, better culture, better support system, better recognition system, better centre or market, better government etc. This is the age of education and learning, this is the age of information and technology, this is the age of intellectual battle. It's a free and open world, globalization and technology makes it more open and free. Human beings are free and contemplative, they are individual and independent. Peoples are finding and deciding, they are open to progress and better or truth. The education system more progressed or developed, the more powerful it is. People are open to unlearn and relearn, the better education you give, the more you become powerful i.e. education superpower. There is open and global competition, education is the best way to lead the world, to be real superpower.

EDUCATION FACTORY education for economy i.e. productive labor (Communist model), human beings are customized product (personal agenda). Education is workforce manufacturing factory today, human beings are commoditized in education factory of today. Either imposed rigid system or system is such weak that it follows others or populism. Communism exploits, capitalism influence but ultimately human beings are becoming slave. Education is free, open and passionate learning to be an independent individual. Education is not slavery or binding methodological force for personal agenda. Neither inside system open nor outside system supportive to be open.

Either it is misusing in the name of education or creates such situation that education become weak to stand independent strongly. Education create leader (rational or decision making ability) but not labor, education enlighten mind and enhance brain but not trained for slavery or physical labor i.e. slave. The inherent nature or main purpose of education being destroyed and blaming education for all, education became a scam like law and politics today. The education deemed to build human and world in such better way is completely failed. Technology makes some efforts but capitalism kills education. The whole global system stand against education, education became paper piece or rituals. There is no educated leader but educated labor, neither human nor education is free in this world. Peoples are the slave of the system, they lost ability to lead or create or think. Everything is commodity in the world includes human beings, system ruling the world but not human being. For a better and efficient education system the world needs a better political system or least healthy environment, first needs basic systemic change for better education. Education cannot change the world from this complete opposite stage, it needs to make neutral for education to work. There shall need a balanced inside and outside effort for a better education.

Education has been always 'regular higher or elite class' (reserved) practice, educated are belongs to politically (rich) and religiously (Brahman caste) higher class but education does never holds or builds extraordinary personality, it always develops ordinary disciplined job class. Education does never create great leader or make government, it creates servant or assistant i.e. government employee. Education has its own limitations, it does not hold creator or leader but caretaker or follower. Education is regular or ordinary or limited selfish class traits, education is not the greatest or superlative. Education is easy and safe way of living ordinary life, it is not fight or risk for revolution or renaissance. Education is civilized, disciplined and hardworking or smart officer training system. The leader or the greatest or the superlatives are not live or born from here, they create or decide or rule the all includes education. So, education is not the one and only platform to learn or lead but a good and popular effort within its limit. Education does not defines the fate of the world, who defines the education they defines the fate of the world and mostly they does not owe the education. Education neither decides your future not guarantee of success, education is always only your assistant or waiting room. Education does not create or provide anything, it only manage or follow your orders. Education follow or assist human instinct only, human born with instinct and they have to follow it. Education does never create or change human instinct, it assist or follow only.

Education is open learning system and training is limited for servitude. Education does never trained or tamed, education is not slave support system but human support system. Training is indoctrination and customization, education is description and universalization. Training dictate and human followed, education support and human decide or creates. Training fixes others agenda through brainwashing to make you weak and dependent, education set own agenda through reasoning to be strong and independent. Training for rule, education for service. Training is blind to exploit, education is light to explore. Training kills, education lives.

Education is not to follow others but follow yourself as who you are, education is not conversion but creation of own way. Education is not to make everyone like me but support everyone to be who they are, education is not a production house of robot but support system of human being. Education is not religious or political agenda, it is secular and educational agenda. Education is open and universal, it is not limited and blind. Education is complete life and daily activity, its real or practical and ordinary or relevant. Education shows the ways for a great journey towards your destination, education is not the destination but ways.

It is human to decide that education or scam, human can make the education worst thing ever in the history. Either in mask or in open can be defined or used education as they wish in their own manner, education can be communalized or corrupt as they wish, the title can be used for personal agenda or scamming. It is human in ultimate who can save education and destroy education, in the name of education they can terrorized future generation. Education has its inherent nature, the politicized or communalized or personalized corrupt things attached with are not education. Education describes and analyzes the world status independently or systematically, it is open and universal. Education is not brainwash or propaganda machine for anything, if anything such happens in the name of education is not education but heinous and darkest hour for the civilization. Education developed by the human beings for their own betterment, it is human to protect it and keep better for everyone's better. Human can make it great or worst, it is human to decide what and how they destroy or protect or respect. Education is not education at all. There needs to be checked and conscious. There are politics in education, business in education, communalism in education, corruption in education, sexual abuse in education but there is no education in education only. [*for instance* Communist Party of China and Education]

Economy improves education or makes education better, education for sustainable economy. Solvency gives stability that process information (lessons of poverty) into knowledge, as much as financial stability human beings have they use more reason to get wisdom. Historically economic development is directly connected to educational development, the world gets develop economically the education develop accordingly. Economy first in human world, then come education. For better education, first better economy and then better education builds sustainable economy with geometric growth. Education is luxury for poor, education cannot create economy independently but it contributes greatly. Without economy there is no education, without education there is economy. Both are interdependent, the more developed economy the more developed education. Education build great economy or make great growth in a sustainable manner, education is not independent but economy is. Economic development contributes towards quality education, education take the economy at a higher and sustainable growth. Economy and education are core centre of the world and human life, it covers and completes human life or makes human life worthy. THAT'S ALL.

Overrated education to decide social status and certify or reserved white-collar careers only. Education does not decide or certify anyone's talent or attitude, it may help a bit to improve things better. Education does not guarantee anyone's character or job, neither decide anyone's status or careers. Individual himself shall build his social status or make him qualified to get white-collar job, education does not guarantee or certify anyone's social status or careers. Education is ordinary process of learning to think and decide better, educated are not special. No one is more or less special in this world, everyone is same and equal. Education does not make someone king or GOD that he can do only white-collar job, today educated are highly corrupt and idiots in the world. Education cannot give character certificate or job guarantee, it is individual who has to earn it through his hard-work and values or attitudes. Education will help in this journey but not decide or guarantee.

IDEA

Education is neither revolutionary nor result based process, the inherent nature of education is to assist or support someone (within its limit) by describing situation and providing supporting environment to think or act on it i.e. lecture and discussion, research and critical thinking, co-curricular and field activities. Education does not decide, it describe only. Education try to address or cover personal and professional needs or emotional intelligence (EQ i.e. emotion or attitude and ethics or values) and intelligence (IQ i.e. intelligence or knowledge and skill). It tries to combine quality with morality. Education wished to build an individual for a happy and worthy or meaningful life through highest or best utilization of his potentials.

Education systems are generalized and specialized, it includes natural, ideal and real contents as curriculum in a easy understandable manner. The ideas or innovation that creates mass impact and recognized by the people in a positive manner are the filtered contents for education system. It is presenting and analyzing in a fundamental or deep and broad or holistic approach. Education system covered the contents in three phases- IDEAL which is primary or elementary education for 7-15 years old i.e.

personal development or interests (literacy, history, identity, dignity, freedom, family, society, culture, language, discipline, mathematics, science, religion etc.) [**IDEAL SCHOOL**], REAL/practical which is secondary and tertiary education for 15- 25 years old i.e. professional development or interests (politics, economy, world system, specialization etc.) [**PROFESSIONAL COLLEGE**] and NATURAL which is higher education for 25 years old to until death i.e. others development or larger interests (wisdom or humanity for contribution, truth, justice, death etc.) [**NATURAL UNIVERSITY**]. The state government may provide a model curriculum for generalized and take a model curriculum from specialized in accordance with government standard. The system shall not include following-

- No vulgarity
- No misinformation or disinformation
- No hate speech
- No political or religious propaganda
- No violation of the law of the land
- No personal attack
- No threat or force or harassment in any forms
- No decision, only description

The curriculum contents shall be progressive (ahead of time i.e. innovative), developed (smart i.e. sensible and practical) and civilized (sensible and calm or gentle i.e. no aggression, no force). Misconceptions or superstitious or unscientific any kind of discriminatory, disrespectful, harmful, inhuman and undignified (indignity) practices or rituals or manners or approaches or concepts i.e. content of curriculum shall be excluded and prohibited or declared illegal like any kind of casteism or racism.

MODEL and **PRACTICAL** learning environment or culture, the school, college and universities will be designed as court, company, lab, library, conference room etc. Each class will have relevant library to study and ask question to teacher, study is voluntary job of student and teacher is there to guide him or show him the way or encourage him to sit in library to study or teach him how to study or answer the students question if they do not understand anything. Teachers are not here to policing or forcing but to answer the question of student to guide or make them think (library format or model education). There will be no class time limit, teacher is the supreme authority over his class and his decision is final. Each course will have a customized large conference room with attached to incumbent teacher office, anyone can join and learn any course, and it will be open course system. Students may take discipleship as enrollment in course, disciple or enrolled shall follow the instructions only (Gurukul). There will be no entrance exam, everyone has right to learn in free of cost. Student can admit and get ID card, student data will be saved in central server and student cannot take or have admission in more than one institution in same time but he can change institution 3 times in a regular manner for lifetime, otherwise he has to file special application and reasonable fees will be charged. There will be no defined class system or grades or year limit, it is open and free or universal. There will be no exam, no grades, and no certificates. Certification business shall stop, certification or formalities shall not barriers in progress of people. Everyone has right to make unlimited attempt for any job irrespective of formal education or academic background by following other requirements like fees, there will be no age limit or attempt limit but fees will be charged for conducting attempt. The authority has discretionary power to accept or reject but no one shall stop or exclude to attempt. No one forced to take education, no one fail or stopped by education. A world of opportunities, a world of push for progress. Teacher may take assessment in any forms and student may participate or not, teacher may share his student's attendance yearly with a personal observation or statement but it will never affect to students anything. The teacher will be highly qualified, highly paid, and the most powerful in the education arena. Teachers rule, teachers decision and teacher in or out i.e. teacher may take any action immediate against students includes suspension from the class or whole institution for temporary or permanent period. Teachers will be advised or administered by senior policy makers i.e. HOD or ED in hierarchy, their job will be reassessed or reevaluate yearly like as private job and seniors or higher authority can take any action immediate includes termination. Teaching will be performance based job, performance will decide promotion or termination. Any complaint or investigation against teacher shall take seriously but conduct respectfully and dignifiedly, teachers shall be trust. There shall be maintained check and balance. The education and system is public that controlled by the government, the institution shall be regulated under the ACT for any misconduct which will be considered as grievous and serious. The government shall conduct the central exam to appoint teachers at all level and government shall conduct yearly reassessment or reevaluation for all, government reserved the exclusive right to terminate teachers. The whole educational infrastructures or campus i.e. school/college/universities or medical or engineering or others specialized shall be established or situated in one place for 7-25 years old or until death to connect dreams from childhood, existing universities can establish school or college building and for 3-5 lakhs people minimum 1 public institutions shall be established. There can be limited government monitored private institution or separate 7-15 years old public school for distance issues if necessary but quality or standard of public institution shall be maintained higher than all others. Sessions will be yearly, curriculum content and classes schedule will be created and published by teacher in public under his office or online portal. It is an invitation from light...

Historically in the ancient wisdom, by respecting freedom of choice there was a culture or standard of living and structure of the society or order or discipline. There were distinct roles for men and women in the society, men were tasked with providing for the family and women were expected to manage households and care for children. Although girls were not provided with formal education but they were required to learn or know (separate non-formal education) a large part of the subject areas to prepare them to maintain the home after marriage, and to educate the children before the age of seven. Family was the fundamental cultural norm and social institution, it was recognized as the fundamental unit of the society, culture, state and the foundation of the human civilization.

Why education? What is the purpose of education? Why need the formal education to acquire knowledge and skill? Whether formal education is only a certificate business? Is education is certification or knowledge? Can anyone or anything certify or measure human potentials? Is this certificate business scam by the company or hypocrisy by the consumer? Whether human beings are taking education for certificate only but in the mask or shield of knowledge? Whether truth is education for earnings, not knowledge? The world has made 'certification system (scam) for earning', people are getting stuck into this scam. In the era of globalization and technology, education or learning is highly accessible that can do anyone by own or individually and independently but 'certification scam' monopoly is the biggest barriers to proceed in/on the way. Neither certification work for companies nor it work for human potentials but in middle few demons are maximizing profit through misusing this system and suppressing or destroying the progress of human civilization. This certification does not define or deliver anything or nothing but a biggest scam of the human history and biggest barriers of human progress. Teaching or learning can be charged (in college) but certification is way of doing business that severely hindrance to the human progress and it does not create any value. Certification in education is just a vacuum, void, valueless, and scam only. Companies are often complaining that certificates does not match with candidates talents, everyone says certificates does not define talents, then why this (certificate) barriers of learning for only few demons profit through killing human progress? Why this certificate? What value it is creating? It is fine for food or medicine, but for education or human potentials it is only the biggest barriers or discouragement or devaluation of learning and suppressed or killed the human progress by the few demons for maximizing profit only. This is the biggest scam by the companies, this is the biggest hypocrisy by the people. One has created this scam, another just following it with false hope but when reality does not match and public became suicidal. People are just crying with the bundle of these valueless certificates for no reason, they are playing blame game for condolence and dying. The companies throwing out them and certificates are just silent, the crowd of 'certificate unemployed' are increasing only. It is about talents, certificate does not create any independent value. What is the value of certificate? Why the companies even made it entry requirements while it does not decide or make any differences? The simple and plain that criteria is talent, where this certificate is coming from there? Here is only talent work, and certificate has no relation with talent. What certificates are doing here? Who do not owe certificate mostly they are ruling the world and 'certificate people' are following them as idol, even if any 'certificate character' create something, no one even care for his certificate or even himself does not give credit to certificate. So, what certificates is doing here in education and learning or talents? Stupid manipulation and scamming...make people stupid to maximize profit only. The funny joke is that neither certificate works in marriage nor in market, certificate is deceiving and scamming in everywhere either in marriage or in market all. Talents finds talents, stupid finds certificates.

Theology is the most ancient discipline in education, the founding department or courses of educational institutions. The religion gave birth education, education ignorant about religion today. Who completed higher education, he does never study a single scriptures whole of any religion including his own but he often made or gave verdict on religion of own or others. A person spend decades after decades in education, he is ignorant about the most ancient, most powerful, most efficient human system in the human history and civilization of the world. The system is ruling the world and human from the time immemorial, the architect of civilization and father of all human system or inventions religion is unknown to him. Religion decides, religion rule and all the time or whole life live or lead under religion but there are severe absence of study religion. Education does not decide, it describe only. Religion is powerful and ancient human system, like other it shall be studied deeply and secularly as human system. It can be read as human book or human system, not god's book or god's system. It can be read with god and without god, system of religion and concept of god are different notion. Religion and God can be read distinctively or independently or separately and also both can be read togetherly or interdependently or connectively. From the time immemorial it is a highly powerful and efficient human recognized system predominantly there in the world, if it has something better or beneficial in anyway then it should study, finds and utilize. Education shall be universal and inclusive, education shall not be the first stair of ignorance and it shall describe in a holistic approach. Neither education shall do religionization nor shall make it religionlessness, education has its inherent nature or basic structure that it may be more influenced by the ages but it never compromised or loses its universality and inclusivity. The inherent nature or basic structure of education is its existence, it never decides but it describes and it describe in a holistic approach. Education is neither propaganda machine nor brainwashing. When I was studying history of education I recurrently failed to ignore the great presence of religion in the history of education, I was afraid to point this out but I felt it is ignorance and in the book of education I cannot be ignorant.

One of the fundamental problems with religion is that theory and practice has huge difference, scriptures and followers are very different. Religion itself secular and universal, in practice followers make it extreme and rigid. Concept of religion independently gets misused less than concept of GOD, people in the name of GOD become over enthusiastic or extreme and superstitious or delusional or hypocrite. Religion is all about inclusivity, followers practiced it exclusivity. It is busy to convert people or make devotee than service to the mankind or welfare. Religion is light but devotees make it dark or make people blind, religion is enlightenment but followers make it ignorance. Religion is democracy, followers used it for dictatorship. Religion is not brainwashing machine, it is critical thinking. The followers practice of extremism, exclusivity and rigidity or dictatorship kill the religion in field. The religion has born for human, when humanity dies then religion dies. When salvation or devotion became more important than service, in the cover of humanity when different agenda try to fulfill then religion die. Religion is independent enough to create impact as it is real witness, allow religion to work rightly and independently. The mass followers make religion fearful or rigid or delusional, religion can't breathe. Don't judge religion by its followers, it is only Holy Scriptures to study and decide. The world needs great support from the most ancient, most powerful, most efficient human system in the human history and civilization of the world- religion. Religion is freedom, not slavery. Read it.

Law is another most ancient discipline i.e. education field invented first in the most of the civilization, law has born before education in the human history. Education codifies and formalized the law, law was in the form of education in ancient time. Primarily, education was all about character building or personality development or moral sense development, law is positive and supportive to the same. Law is nothing but common sense, consciousness, conscience and the ultimate goal of the education is same. Law is the guiding light of the society or social order, education is enlightening the society. Law is about reason and critical thinking of society or understanding society, education describes society and critical thinking of the society. Law is codification of human practice and custom or regulation of individual and institution, education is the description and analysis of law and its broad background. Law regulate human or global issues, education describe the human or global issues. Law and education both are the civilizing forces, law is deciding rules and principles where education is critical discussion of it. Education contributes in the legal development, law educate the people and education makes law efficient than fear. Law and education both ensures rational or critical thinking of human being, both covers the larger canvas of the world. Education minimize the necessity of law, law may support sometime in need. Where law is not necessity but education works, that is truly civilized. Law is primitive, education is modern and civilized. Law is problem, education solution and the ultimate goal of law is to educate people. The more education works the less law will work. Law is last, education is first. If education failed, law will be failed definitely. Law can be a temporary injunction, education is the sustainable solution. Therefore, such standard education shall be required which will decrease the necessity of law. If the efficiency of education will increase, the necessity of law will decrease. Law is the one way to educate people, education covers all includes law. Education and system can build a great world together.

Military education and training is important part of the curriculum for all the citizens above 15 years of age in every institution which can be conducted by the regular or retired army officials of the state, once in a week day long training shall be practiced regularly and strictly. A global standard of physical fitness and confidence can be supported by education, body and mind both are equally important for a great living which is recognized and aims of education to support it. Education provides a complete preparation to make a life worthy, it aims to develop citizen individual and independent. Body is the real existence and fuel of life, without military training education is incomplete. It can be studied as course that covers theory and practice, anyone at anytime above 15 years of age can join voluntarily without any force. State may make it compulsory in a separate program but education cannot make anything compulsory till you joined or consented for something. You have right to not join class, if you join class then you have to follow the discipline or decorum of the class that instructed by teacher. Military education and training is not mere physical exercise, it is hard core professional training and course.

Crisis creates leader, self- respect and fearless stand complete the leadership. The slave of empire and fearful scholars are just commodity in the market, they cannot create or lead nothing in the world. The truth and true scholars are being targeted by the empire in the history, scholars have the inherent responsibility to fight and guide the people in hard times. The scholars shall not be commoditized products in the market, the collaborators of injustice caused by the state. Scholar can never be silent and escaped away from the crisis, they stand and fight till the death against wrong or injustice. The self- respect and fearless stand is synonymous to the scholar, scholars are the true enlightened and ultimate hope for the oppressed in bad regime. The real scholar can never limit or exclude himself from the situation in anyway, he shall fight with his highest possible capacity. Scholars are the light of hope in the darkest hour of the civilization, hope for the ship caught in the huge danger of storm. Scholars are the wind of change, they do not follow the wind only. Though in normal situation scholar describes the issues but in the crisis scholar decides the way, in war zone everyone is soldiers.

Teacher based education system i.e. monastery or gurukul or teachers centre, who is teacher? Teachers are the centre of education, teacher is education, and teacher is institution. Education is not infrastructures or business management where teachers are daily labor or staff, which is certificate business only. All the uneducated real estate characters build or make buildings and named it educational institution which gets licensed by the government also. They do real estate business, student or education are all commodity for them and they hired staff or daily labor named teacher. They commoditized the whole thing like real estate, they make education is all about management or business management. It is a management business, a certificate business, and biggest scam or hypocrisy. There are no teacher, there are daily labor called staff only. Teacher born one in centuries, others are staff only to run the institutions regular clerical works. Education is not mere employment, education is enlightenment. Teacher is not job post title, it is an attitude and character or personality. It is not about life, it is more about death. Education is not about management and buildings, education is teacher and teacher is education. In the name of teacher a staff or clerk or labor class has been developed, this corrupt government (political party) servant or corporate clerk will be found in all the corruption and saving the interest of government or corporate. Neither they are wise nor honest, they are murderers of nation or civilization in the disguise of teacher. Socrates is the teacher who accepts the death for truth, government servant or corporate servant is servant only. Teaching is life but not lectures, teacher is ideology but not mere corporate job.

Parents or aged members of the communities were teacher in the ancient period, it was not formal profession or institutional occupation. Gradually the concept of teacher has been evolved professionally, who has experienced or expertise in the specific field they were start to teach formally or institutionally. Teacher was not salaried staff, they were independent and it owes high social status. Teacher was not so available and cheap, teacher was idol or ideology. Teacher was not mere lecture, teacher was complete life. Teacher was truth and wise, teacher was not slide presenter or information transmitter only like today which is replacing by internet or AI. Teaching is an attitude, it has huge impact or influence on others life. The spirit of teaching or the wisdom in teaching has been consistently missing in last 2-3 centuries of the world. This has became commoditized or corporatized, the clerks and machines are running education institution. The soul or spirit of the teaching has dead, it does not have any impact or influence on human life today. It became a clerical job to sell and deliver certificates, the attitude and dignity is no more. One of the most fake and failed entity in the human civilization is the teacher today. Teachers are the foundation of education, the concept of education has been developed rapidly in unplanned and immatured manner where the foundation has been missing or so weak. The class of teacher has not been grown or evolved or developed, education became a cool populist agenda. Finally, education became commodity where clerk became teacher.

If anyone is qualified enough to be a teacher, he shall get the highest financial package. A teacher shall not need to think about financial crisis, the main concern for a teacher is to get high qualifications. A teacher shall exclusively devoted or dedicated his life in teaching and research, a teacher shall not be engage in any other business or money making corporate machine i.e. trader shall not be teacher. A teacher shall be the idol for the disciple, a living ideology for all. The state shall create such system or environment that qualified teacher need not think about money, they would be honored and considered in highly prestigious field. The most genius and greatest personality of the nation shall be in teaching, neither teacher nor state shall make money important before teaching. Teacher shall be teacher by choice, not by chance or by profession. Teaching is not regular job or profession, teaching is attitude and ability i.e. born to teach. Trader shall not be teacher, teacher shall not have to think for money. Teacher is the guiding light for the nation, state shall give free hand budget for them and for education.

Office politics or unprofessionalism in teaching fraternity is very dangerous, it destroys the education and academic environment. It creates existential crisis for an educational institution, it kills space to think or research. It severely affects life of students and institutions, it cultivates ignorance and kills genius. Unprofessionalism among teachers and with students is the biggest enemy of education and educational institutions, it is barbarism in education. The education and research institution shall be calm and gentle, respectful and dignified, patience and tolerance, formal and professional, dialogic and broad, open and free, intellectual and civil, emotionally intelligent etc.

PEDAGOGY is not only how to teach but also how to learn, how to learn guided how to teach. Pupils learn through different way like reading or analyzing, listening or connecting, communicating or debating, writing or doing or observing or creating etc. and shall encourage open or independent minds i.e. "I may disagree with what you say, but I will defend to the death your right to say it"- Voltaire. The ways or method of teaching shall be in relevant or popular tools and connecting or touching with feelings, tools or way that connect feelings or relate or awake mind is the best way to teach. It can be poetically or dramatically or musically or religiously or emotionally or intellectually or contextually or comparatively with example or statistically with data or facts or information etc. Though all the ways are itself independent subject or faculty but the subjects and methods of teaching are interdependent or interrelated one to another. Education shall be connective or relatable and enjoyable or easily understandable. For instances, teaching in mother tongue, objective and eloquent presentation, Socratic method etc. and can be established teaching institute or college or department of education. Teacher shall be highly professional and get high moral personality, strong morality creates a spiritual connects or impact. The academic intellect and emotional intelligence or administrative skills both are equally important in teaching to make it work, understands students problems individually and patiently giving efforts to make it better is considered a good teacher. A great thought provoking relevant question paper or examination system and paper checking or activity findings is also a great teaching or learning for the students. Everyone has own style of teaching, but the teaching shall describe or analyze subjects to make understand and to make think. It shall be understands enough that hit on to think on it seriously, understanding description and analysis to think. So, teaching shall ensure two things that- 1) it describes and analyze in an unbiased manner or holistically, it never decides and worship or bias 2) it shall be understandable and thoughtful. The final maxim is- teachers are not GOD, they are not supreme or absolute in intellect or knowledge and emotion or morality which shall keep in mind always for both teacher and students or whole education community. Education does not cover everything at best way, education does not decide life. It has limitations and problems, it is a supporting tool like many others to make possible efforts to make the world and human life better. BE AWARE!

Discipline in class, discipline in life, and discipline in education make things great. One of the main purposes of the education is to create, build and maintain discipline. Discipline is safe, wise and productive learning. Discipline is strict but focused, discipline is force or power but beneficial. It is serious and necessary in the classroom, without discipline there is no education. A healthy environment makes great impact on learning, education is attitude or personality and sensibility. Discipline is must for learning environment, discipline is another name of formal education. Discipline for system or culture or environment of education, no force or discipline for study or home task or learning. You may not be present in the class, if you present in the class then you have to be disciplined. You have the right to not study or follow the lectures, you do not have any right to be notorious or disturb the class in any form of behavior. Discipline in action, not in thought.

Examination for progress, not for regress and examination shall not be certification but suggestions to improve. Examination is attempts and the purpose is to check or review the ability or improvements. It shall not be hindrance to human progress, it shall not be limited or create long gap to waste time. Examination shall be frequent, available, convenient, progressive and limitless attempt. It shall not be illusion or godly or untouchable, overrated, expensive, fear, and failure. Exam shall not be imposed or enforced, it shall be spontaneous or voluntary. Fail in exam does not certify anything, it shall not be standard of anything and it shall not waste time that hindrance to human progress. Examination is not certification, it does not certify or guarantee anyone's ability or talent. It is checking weight after everyday gym only, EXAMINATION MEANS **"KNOW THYSELF"**. It's a way to understand, it is not correct or absolute all the time. So, it may support human progress but it does not decide, it's a way to know but not final outcome. Examination is not independent quality or ability or guarantee etc.

Research institute or academy can be established privately or publicly and patronaged by the state or others for development and creation of knowledge, educated and experienced expert can be distinguished member of the academy. They will open the diversified doors of knowledge, their creation would be the part of curriculum. They will conclude the various description and analysis, they will decide on wisdom sometime. This is the category of decision or judgment, a specialized place for innovation and creation. Imagination, intuition, experimentation, observation, codification, innovation, creation, wisdom etc. are the fundamental characteristics of the academy. It is not truth, it is content of curriculum that hits you to think. It is not part of formal education, it is independent and one kind of profession or passion. Each academy has specialization, philosophy or art or science as like company. They create and sale to the individual or state, quality product has more sale and recognition. It contributes or supports in the development of education directly, there can be academy for education to ensure quality education. It can be part of the education in curriculum or it can sometime decide the nature or scope of education, education never decides but describes and analyze only.

Research is relevant and contemporary discovery or innovation for the common good of humanity. It enriches individual thoughts and contributes sustainable solution for the larger interests. If anyone asks the question that where education wants to go or reach? The simple answer is to research, research mind, and environment of research, culture of research, resources of research and capacity of research. Education aims at enhancing research, education purpose is to build research mind, analytical ability or critical thinking. Education is not mere teaching, teaching for pushing you to think. Research is authentic way of converting information into knowledge or wisdom, rationalize (input) and humanize (output) decision. Research for practical thinking or smart work, education make efforts to build a worthy life that peaceful and secured. Education provides resources or research materials before you to react or act on it, to observe or think and decide or work on it. Research scholarship or incentive to the innovation shall needs to be a culture in a state, the sufficient and available research or innovation budget is key to sustainable development. Education system shall allocate more resources and budget on research, otherwise there will be no education but scam and scam only.

Co-curricular activities are open and free the birds from cage to fly, here you found the beautiful and musical voice of birds. It is not occasional part of education, it is regular practice of education. To accomplish education is largely includes co-curricular activities, it enhances practical capacity in building vision. A quality way of education is co-curricular activities, it includes different clubs and competitions, sports and cultural activities, research and activism etc. It covers wisdom and skills, it works for quality and skill development through personal and professional clubs i.e. debate, diplomacy, language, culture, research, literature, GK, think tank, social welfare, sports, entertainment, job, admission, IT, professional specialized like doctor, engineer, lawyer, academicians, journalist, businessmen etc. that connects to build Analytical ability, Management skill, Communication skill, Convincing power, Team work and Decision- making power, Diplomatic ability and Negotiation skill, Language skill, Accountability management, Professionalism etc. It completes education, it creates leader. All the co-curricular activities generally practiced in classroom under curricular activity, co-curricular specialize and practice more interestingly.

Students and teachers shall enjoy certain immunities and privileges such as protection against unjust arrest, right to fair trail, dwell in security, protection against extortion in financial dealings, right to strike, discontinue lectures, protest against grievances or interference with established rights, easy accessibility to the public resources, necessary research fund, provide special incentive and necessary employment support to the graduates, priority in government service and schemes, special legal protection and security against any issues or conflicts etc. They shall feel special or important and dignified or respected by the state, they shall have the courage to challenge and they shall never feel inferior or neglected. They shall have the liberty to fail and fight for his decision, they shall get the things done. They shall own the country, they feel the country. They shall get a pure soul, highest utilize their potentials and build a worthy life. They are the face of the world, vision of the world and they shall get that love and care or respect what the world expect from them.

Library in education or education in library and technological impacts or online library, library is the more accessible, more available and more affordable information and knowledge house. Library is the face or identity or instinct of the education, education is library that describes and analyzed by teacher. Library is the collection, documentation and translation centre to make knowledge available broadly which address given by teacher to make disciple think. Though teacher is library and institution but library buildings are the place of study and think deeply. Education is teacher, education in library. Where disciple attracted or addicted to library but not notes photocopy, where disciple study and ask question to think but not memorize syllabus is education.

A child shall start his formal education at the age of 7 where he shall not be taught or trained (i.e. socialization or enculturation) anything but allow to be natural grown up till 10-12 years of age at least to get the ability to use of reason and he shall never be in hostel or boarding before 19 years old age which is time for family education as family responsibility. The state shall make available, affordable and accessible quality education considering the family residence. Education for life and happiness, education is not for killing childhood or adulthood that irrecoverable but regrettable for whole life. Family is the best school and teacher for life, family touch and family education is the ultimate foundation of life. The love and care of the family makes man gem, there is no better education than this and without this education no education would work ever. The professional knowledge or understanding would start after 19 years old, this will be focused or specialized for professional world. Now, he can take the way, fight for what he want or need. Before 19 years old separation of children from the parents is crime against humanity, he will destroy the humanity and no education will work on him. Wherever children were at the day but at night and dinner shall be at home with parents together is the greatest education. Love begets love, hate begets hate and education or everything for love. If you have to send him boarding school, don't take babies, its crime.

Infrastructures or buildings or classrooms shall be clean, calm and wide. It shall not be party centre or club, it shall not be public picnic spot or public programs or noisy public meetings venue. Infrastructures shall be simple and separate with wide space, it shall be necessity but not luxury. It shall be comfortable and more natural than artificial buildings, the facilities or design shall be humble and respectful. Infrastructure is not big buildings or machines, it is simple and natural environment. It shall be designed in a manner so that resources can easily available in one place and capacity to resolve issues at own area. Buildings shall not stop sky, light shall not stop sun or stars. It may have some artistic works, it shall not be paint shop or museum or movie theatre. It is an educational institution, it is neither real estate companies corporate office nor five star luxury hotel. It is not slave production house, it offers wisdom and human dignity. It is original and natural, it is not fake and hypocrisy. It describes the accurate and authentic, it does not exaggerate or limit. It is free or natural flow, it is neither influences nor brainwash. It owes meditative or spiritual nature to the some extent, it is neither picnic spot nor program venue or party centre. It is not factory or production house, it is calm and quiet GOD'S office to observe complete or whole and to decide future of the world. This is GOD'S abode.

An efficient monitoring system can be developed, administration monitor teacher and teacher monitor students. Teacher can be reassessed or professionalism can be monitored strictly, unnecessary interferences or student evaluation is serious stupidity. It is not corporate house that customer is ranking company or staff, today institutions are became a corporate house where the pure environment of education is absent. The foundation of educational institution the respect and dignity has completely lost, the impact of education severely decreased. The monitoring system shall be healthy and efficient, it shall be encouraging and positive. A culture of education shall be developed, professionalism shall not be compromised. Teacher can advice individual student or can consult with parents of the students together. Teacher can observe and make report to share with individual student, teacher act on it independently.

Public administration of education under legislation, ministry, division board, central commission, district or sub-district offices etc. efficient functioning are very important for quality education, inexperienced or ignorant bureaucracy or authority strongly discourage the education minds. The sincere and sensible cooperation from the administration encourage education minds, it creates a necessary exclusive environment for education. Administration of educational institution shall be free from professional or personal office politics, the experienced teacher shall not be busy in regular class schedule but in policy making and administration only. Politicization of administration is deep and destructive, in education it is like life in danger. Education has its inherent instinct and exclusive environment to work, political bias or communalism is dangerous for health of education. Education covers politics, education shall not be politicized. It is better to run the administration through relevant and inside individuals.

Ministry or commission for education is the state recognition of importance of education and its impact. All states are today giving high priority in education, it is top five agenda of state. There are many specialized ACT, department, commission, ministry, programs, funds have been created by the state. Various international organization works seriously for ensuring quality education, education is the prime global agenda today for enhancing human capacity to the best utilization of human potentials. Education capability or availability or accessibility is more important than compulsory education slogans, education shall not be forceful but available or accessible or affordable for interested one. Education shall be free, open and passionate learning. Build education culture, education environment, education value and system.

Free education or public education or government education, peoples are paying tax and they shall not direct or separate pay for education. Education is basic need and fundamental right, it is state or government fundamental responsibility to manage and expense for education. Equality in education and health, equitable distribution of resources are founding pillars of state. If any citizen of state deprived or discriminated in education and health, demand and necessity of quality education and health for all equally if not fulfilled then this is not state or failed state. State has born to ensure basic necessity of citizen irrespective of any grounds to make them minimum capable individual and independent where education is primary. If state failed to serve its founding purpose, then there is no need of state for to only pay huge amount to maintain it as because other institution or individual is enough capable to manage their own other affairs. Education is the primary capacity and service of the state to all the citizens equally. State is a collective efforts and equitable resource distribution. State shall protect and serve the citizen so that citizen can do same to the state. To become a state it shall fulfill minimum conditions.

State shall offer one and single secular standard model education to its citizen, it is always open and free. No one will be forced, everyone has to take education as per his choice. Anyone can open and run educational institution maintaining the government standard, exclusively for educational purpose which approval is on absolute government discretion without further questions. State shall not support or recognize any other educational institution except public education, state shall not support or promote any specialized education like memorizing religious scriptures in religious institutions or places. State shall have the one secular education system which supported by government, any other specialized education shall be regulated by government but without any support or recognition or promotion.

Education and politics are very connected to each other, education shall be free from power politics or party ideologies but it never happened. Politics always use the education as tools to brainwash and use as propaganda machine of personal agenda. The change of government change the policies for education, education became a party programs. Education is customized labour factory as per government convenience, instruments to train slave for party ideology. From the policies to administration all of education extremely politicized by the government, education became lie factory or corrupt political party agent. Public education lost people's faith on it, people has reasonable or potential fear about public education. It is alarming, way to Dark Age. The content, curriculum and teacher or staff or administrations are politicized and corrupted by government. Education supports to seek truth, public education fake truth and corrupt brain. Education became a personal daily social media vlogs or government magazine, legal tools to brainwash for personal ideology. Education is Goebbels class, a licensed propaganda machine. Education needs to be free and independent, it shall be secular and universal. Education shall be inclusive and impartial or unbias, it shall describe and analyze broadly or holistically. Education shall never be corrupt and bias, it shall be centre for free thinking. Education cultivates rational mind, it never manufacture ignorant mind or blind believers. Education is the backbone of nation, politics is the servant of the education. Education guide politics, if politics control education then the nation will be controlled and chained for slavery forever. Education is light, if anyone or anything off the light means dark night starts. One of the main purpose of politics is to protect and promote quality education, to serve and work for education independently.

Private coaching centers or home tutoring is grievous failure of public education system and ruthless torture for students. It is financially and educationally or intellectually over burden for parents and students. It destroys the importance and faith on public education system, it creates an education corruption hub. It is unnatural, it is forceful. It is the biggest barriers in natural exploration of human potentials, it is national artificial autism production factory. Home tutoring may be permissible for any special or vocation purpose within limited period, it shall not be national culture in beside or together public education system. It is either failure of the public education system or over competitive parental pressure, both are dangerous and seriously disturbing. Education is free flow spontaneous and boundless tools, it does not certify or decide anyone's life. Moreover, the failure of the system necessitate the alternative, the system shall be efficient and high standard place of public faith so that no alternative shall necessitate to stand against him.

Education shall not be pressure or curriculum shall not be over excessive load turns into intolerable burden, it shall be simple and interesting to relate and progress in future. Early age schooling and put over burden on their shoulders is inhuman and unscientific. Freedom of learning or liberty to learn is being snatched from the very early age of a child, they put into a pressure cooker for boiling but they melted to become bad smelled soup. A forceful system with huge burden just put on a child without considering his interest or passion, either he has to finish it in limited time or he will be declared failure or looser. There so much of things or subjects or activity put on him that he cannot even figure out anything in severe confusion and pressure. There shall be discipline with liberty, dignity with decision and freedom with passion. The freedom of choice is more important than pass-fail, special interest is preferable than meaningless everything. Education is free flow spontaneous and boundless tools, it does not certify or decide anyone's life. Take time, go with the flow, find yourself, and have fun is the real definition of education. Education follows you, support you and respect your choice but it never decide or dictate you. Education for you, you are not for education. Education shall not disturb or dictate human beings, it shall support or nurture human choice only. Let them decide...

Education in institution only, in library or class but no education shall at home or fields. Institutions are open always, study and learn as you can but do not take pressure at home or out of the campus. No homework or force to study at home or out of campus, it is personal choice where strongly recommended not to study at home or out of campus. It is better to observe, experiment, discuss, understand, stop and think with family, society, relatives etc. out of campus. Relax and refresh your brain, party with family and friends, feel the sun and sky, feel the nature and universe, see the world and human, and study all of them at campus in deep to create or make something. There shall not be boundary of pass-fail or certification, it is more like open credit system that study as you like and may not or may sit for exam whenever you think fit for certification.

Education does not aim at pass-fail or certification in limited time, education is open and free learning system. Education is not skill development training course in limited, it specialize and expertise you on your interest. It is neither certificate delivery system nor anything anyone's certificate can work on human potentials, education supports you to be special and expert on your own way but can never decide or dictate. Your expertise is your ultimate certificate or recognition, all others scam only. This is the practical truth, it should truth in theory or paper of market and state also.

Education cannot have ideology or morality, education cannot be organized religion or political party to terrorize people which is serious crime. Education is not domestic animal training system for taming people, it is unscientific and uneducational. Education is free and open or universal inclusive description and analysis system. Education cannot decide, education do not know anything to decide. There is nothing absolute, let the people decide in their own way by analyzing educational tools or materials. Education can be deciding partner, not decision maker. It is only delivery system, neither it manufacturer nor consumer. The curriculum may have priorities according to time and context, more focus or have some specialization on like religion or science etc. but not extreme biasness or exclusion. Education shall describe and analyze, people shall create and decide that will be recognized and used. Description and analysis does not mean only book reading or slide presentation in class, it is critical and creative or practical and experimental. There shall be experimental and free thinking or creative and critical thinking environment but not brainwash or propaganda of personal agenda. Education does not have any religion or ideology or morality, it is free, open and universal or inclusive.

The introduction of textbooks are political and narrow concept, it is used for brainwash and used to grow up in limited world or narrow corner. The state may set the model curriculum as guideline, get some reference book may be stored under his authority. Textbook is deciding the issues according to governments, invested public money for propagation of personal agenda under the governments. Textbooks are controversial in many countries of the world, it is limited or narrow material. There was a necessity of textbook when information was not available and accessible, now there is no need of textbook in the age of information. Today textbook means political propaganda and shackling the minds of future generation in a limited or narrow circle. Textbook is mental disability, it is killing real education or wisdom or open learning. The state may guide the people through model curriculum, people will decide the way. Textbook is weakness and ignorance, it is textbox of human potentials. It has huge psychological impact, it makes slave only.

Educational institute can do business for its own financial independency through publication, printing, media, research, consultation, conference, technology and innovation, special courses and training, education stationeries etc., education and institution can be saleable. It shall sale exclusively education materials, not other commodities. Education business shall promote education, it must increase the value of intellectual work. This shall not be pure business like other, it shall encourage and contribute in education or academia. The business shall maintain education standard, the main purpose is to get education importance more only. Education is not business, some businesses are education. It is like high bidding for a paint that does never made for business by the artist, the aesthetic value is always more than monetary value. Education can never measured by money, it is always more than that. Education business is not regular business, money cannot measure its value only. It is always a great service.

Equal access to education is state fundamental responsibility and state shall maintain special concern for rural areas or indigenous people, minorities or disadvantaged, child, women, handicapped or disabled, night school for workers or labors etc. The rural and urban differences shall be wiped out in education facilities and policies, both shall have the equal opportunity and facilities with special concern. To ensure equality in all facilities of education may need to work on some external factors like poverty or local issues, need some special arrangements for some class like handicapped or laborers which shall needs to be addressed efficiently to maintain progressive education. Education is not blind or narrow, it is vigilant and universal. Equity in education is precondition to ensure equality, deprivation or backwardness is real enemy of the education. Education is inclusive but not exclusive, no one can be deprived or backward in the eye of education. Education for all, education is everyone's equal right.

Brain drain is dangerous and biggest concern for education, no matter how far quality education you may develop if it does not work for you. The efforts shall make to stop brain drain, either afford him or support him. Improve quality education, improve quality economy and politics. Brain drain or brain dead is not only for employment but also political, cultural, social, religious etc. many other factors are behind it. It is not possible to control absolutely, but it is seriously concerning and shall take necessary possible measures to minimize it at a lower rate.

Dropout problem is not for only educational expenses but for family expenses also, poverty is the root cause of dropout. Free education cannot stop dropout completely, it can decrease a huge number and control with great efficiency. To fight with dropout, the state shall fight with poverty. Poverty reduction will decrease dropout, to give a mid-day meal for one does not fill the stomach of others. Free education in poverty is meaningless, poverty level decrease and education level increase shall run together in a balanced manner.

Inappropriate curriculum and teaching method or culture strongly discourage learning or encourage dropout. It makes learning difficult and disconnected, it pressurize and panic the learner. Inappropriate curriculum and inefficient teacher or teaching methods make things disastrous, it destroy the future of students. They try to force or pressurize on student the wrong thing, student repeatedly failed to get it and dropped out or grade-repeat or take wrong direction. It disturbs and suppress the student or talent, either he dropped out or became a depressed unhappy or unworthy professional. He lost the natural energy to create or build something own great, he lost individuality and became a burden for this planet. Inappropriate curriculum and inefficient teacher or teaching methods kill the dreams and passions of millions, the rigid and forceful wrong education is suicidal for the civilization. Instead of student-centered education subject or rigid curriculum centered forceful education contributing to either dropout or slavery, it is disturbing the global peace. I do not like you but you are forcing me, forcing me in a better way at least. The curriculum is inappropriate that teacher forcing on me in a terrific way.

The things which unnecessary and irrelevant but forcing or pressurizing to take it in a dictating or improper way of terrific teaching is genocidal, overrated education in society and state mechanisms is the greatest burden on human shoulders today. Without education you do not have any space, the education poisonous to you. Freedom of choice and liberty to live a human life is almost impossible in modern world, there are few systems made by some people in sometime and it is absolute. Degree decide life here, system decide death hour. Either be slave of system or out, the individuality and innovation is to make revolution almost. Truth is that who take that risk, they revolutionize the world. But the destructive or slave system does not change, find better excuse to do his job only. Everything is progressing in this world except human dignity or humanity, degree or money measure the human position here in this world. Everything is free except human, thousands of systematic chain tied up human in cage. They are being trained for slavery, trained and untrained slave. Open curriculum, quality and wise teaching is urgent needs for the freedom of education and human beings. The great curriculum can be worst because of poor teaching, quality and wise teaching can make worst curriculum great even. Teaching is the main pillar of education, education stands on great teaching. The teacher shall have excellence in subject, high morals, wisdom and maintain high professionalism. The most brilliant and wise individual shall be teacher, clerk or staff or servant of corporate are not teacher. Without great teacher and recognizes teaching as highly successful profession of all, there will be no education but joke. The more you invest in teaching, the more you get better education. Teacher is education, education is teacher; education is not buildings.

Education is progress, teacher is education. Teacher is the foundation of civilization, future leader.

Human beings are the leaders of the world, the greatest resources on the earth. The more you made human beings better, the more you made the world better. Human beings are the ends of all, they are the ultimate wealth creators and world protectors. They will take the nation and civilization ahead, human reason is the most powerful resources on the earth which decides the fate of the world. The better reasoning will take better decision, it creates and protects. To live and to progress or sustain, human reason is the best and only way that shall be high priority in all policies. Education is the servant of human reason, a great support. So, the governments or states shall support and more invest in education.

INSTANCE

UNIVERSAL DECLARATION ON EDUCATION, 2024
Preamble:

> *'I cannot teach anybody anything, I can only make them think' – **Socrates**.*

> *'If you can't explain it simply, you don't understand it well enough'- **Albert Einstein**.*

1.Definition:

Education is the transmission or description or analysis of world's status before human beings so that human beings can smartly act or react to it.

2.Principle (s):

a. Free, flexible and available one public education system for all.

b. No one forced to take education, no one fail or stopped by education.

c. No certification or time limit

d.   No private coaching centers

3.Aim (s):
To develop citizen individual and independent through delivering inclusive or unbiased and systematic description and analysis of global status.

4.Vision:
Education wished to build an individual for a happy and worthy or meaningful life through highest or best utilization of his potentials.

5.Mission:

a.   Strong family ties and community feelings,
b.   Acceptance of state authority and abide by law,
c.   History, culture and religious understanding, and
d.   Military discipline.

6.Phase (s):
1)-

a.   Elementary or ideal (7 years up),
b.   Tertiary or practical, and
c.   Higher education or natural

2) A child shall never be in hostel or boarding before 19 years old age which is time for family education as family responsibility

7.Method (s):

a.   Study circle,
b.   Lecture,
c.   Practical class,
d.   Public lecture,

e. Q& A,
f. Assignments,
g. Debate and dialogue within universities and between countries,
h. Experimental,
a. Disciplined,
j. Specialized or exclusive care for one to one individual students according to abilities or potentials,
k. Not more than 30-35 students in a class or under a teacher,

8.Qualifications of Teacher:

a. Wise,
b. Expertise and experience (intellect),
c. Eloquence,
d. Attitude,
e. Emotional intelligence,
f. Analytical ability,
g. Administrative skills,
h. Decision making power,
a. Leadership,
j. Professionalism,
k. Understanding human nature,
ax. Minimum age 30-35 years old,

9.Administration:

a. The education system administered through legislation, ministry, division board, central commission, district or sub-district offices, local committees etc.
b. *Administration of educational institution* shall be free from professional or personal office politics, the

experienced teacher shall not be busy in regular class schedule but in policy making and administration only.

c. Education covers politics, education shall not be politicized. It is better to run the administration through relevant and inside individuals.

10. Access to education:

Equal access to education is state fundamental responsibility and state shall maintain *special concern* for rural areas or indigenous people, minorities or disadvantaged, child, women, handicapped or disabled, night school for workers or labors etc.

11. Curriculum:

1) Education systems are generalized and specialized, it includes natural, ideal and real contents as curriculum in a easy understandable manner. The ideas or innovation that creates mass impact and recognized by the people in a positive manner are the filtered contents for education system. It is presenting and analyzing in a fundamental or deep and broad or holistic approach. Education system covered the contents in three phases-

a. IDEAL which is primary or elementary education for 7-15 years old i.e. personal development or interests (literacy, history, identity, dignity, freedom, family, society, culture, language, discipline, mathematics, science, religion etc.) [**IDEAL SCHOOL**],

b. REAL/practical which is secondary and tertiary education for 15- 25 years old i.e. professional development or interests (politics, economy, world system, specialization etc.) [**PROFESSIONAL COLLEGE**] and

c. NATURAL which is higher education for 25 years old to until death i.e. others development or larger interests (wisdom or humanity for contribution, truth, justice, death etc.) [**NATURAL UNIVERSITY**]. The state government may provide a model curriculum for generalized and take a model curriculum from specialized in accordance with government standard.

2) The system shall not include following-

a. No vulgarity
b. No misinformation or disinformation
c. No hate speech
d. No political or religious propaganda
e. No violation of the law of the land
f. No personal attack
g. No threat or force or harassment in any forms
h. No decision, only description

3) The curriculum contents shall be-

a. progressive (ahead of time i.e. innovative),
b. developed (smart i.e. sensible and practical) and
c. civilized (sensible and calm or gentle i.e. no aggression, no force).

4) Misconceptions or superstitious or unscientific any kind of discriminatory, disrespectful, harmful, inhuman and undignified (indignity) practices or rituals or manners or approaches or concepts i.e. content of curriculum shall be excluded and prohibited or declared illegal like any kind of casteism or racism.

12.Environment:

It is not factory or production house, it is calm and quiet GOD'S office to observe complete or whole and to decide future of the world. This is GOD'S abode.

53

ETHICAL i.e. POLITICS

CAPITALISM i.e.

RESOURCES

"**ECONOMY** (management or political economy)*of* **NATURE** (resources or economics)and **DIGNITY** (human or politics)"

CHAPTER II

ETHICAL CAPITALISM

INTRODUCTION

There are three familiar terms monetary (individual i.e. money), finance (institution or organization i.e. monetary activity), economy (state or world i.e. policy and management). Economy is not money but resources, money is one converted exchange form of resources only and finance is monetary activity. Everything of this world can be economic resources, resources are driving forces or fuel of this world and service or needs of mankind. It does not have any color or morality, its religion is absolute power. It controls and decides the fate or future of the world, the 'MANAGEMENT' of the resource is its all. Mismanagement or misuse of the resources caused the greatest threat to the existence of world and human civilization. If mankind is leading the world, resources and its proper management are trust and responsibility upon world leaders. Economy is the central to the state and global systems or mechanisms like politics and government, economy is empire. Resource is not economy, economy is resource management.

Either resources has been created or acquired or earned by the human beings through force or exchange, it is transactional or transferable or convertible. Individual necessity is the driving force of resources and intelligent mind or dealings fixes the winner, necessity has no boundaries. Some of multiply the resources, some of make losses and caused damages of the resources. The resource has become central to conflicts and crises, pain and power or progress. Global population, resources, its importance or control, competition or race and necessity has been increased. The social balance or world order messed up recurrently, human dignity became impossible for the whole mankind. The natural and human disaster creates more tough situation for the world, the world recurrently failing in efficient management of the resources. The situation became extreme and uncontrollable, uncontrollable human weaknesses and resources misuse or imbalance. The world has become a place for impossible fight for living or endless struggle, peace and security is also became an impossible fight. Here economy is trying to improve the situation, rescue the world from disaster and ensure human dignity. Economy is trying to make some efficient resource management policies and systems, innovation or creation and maintain or manages existing resources in a sustainable manner. Economy is the complete study of resources, the whole life of resource born to death and its great or efficient management is the economy. The external and internal all the relevant factors to the resources are the subject matter of the economy, economy is the blueprint for world future. The world has resources more than human needs but it is limited, so the world needs economy. Economy is not mere political concept, it is more social and individual concept. Economy for security, economy for progress.

Resources or economic power does not have color or morality, politics or political power has color or morality which is public good. Politics is public system for public good, it owes the power to regulate all. Politics shall regulate and manage resources, the problem is resources regulating and managing politics. Resources has no character or color or class, it is reckless and dangerous.

Politics is the highest form of power to fulfill human needs in maintaining utmost human dignity, politics for civilizing and humanizing the world. Human beings made the political system with all the power or authority and trust for a better world, but it is all sold out to resources. Resources are the real or super government, political government is just titular government. Resources are reckless and dangerous, it made the human beings most cheap commodity or valueless and politics as comedy circus. Resource can buy and sell everything i.e. truth, justice, dignity etc., it can buy and sell its boss i.e. politics. So, the resources became ruthless oppressor or Frankenstein and heinous criminal of the world, it controls the world. Resources are servant but not leaders, if it became leader that would be disaster. It is like mad dog which is fine in tied, if it is untied then it became reckless and dangerous. Today resources are above human, human worship resources. The dangerous economic rise is the greatest failure of politics and historic disgraceful event for politics. Politics destroy the peace and global resources, it corrupts and kills global economy. Politics is the sole responsible for today's world. Economy may make great efficient resource management policies and system but it implements through politics only, if politics corrupts or sold out then no economy can make progress. A welfare and dignified politics or state can give a welfare and dignified economy. Economic prosperity is much celebrated for human beings, human beings are not for economy or not controlled by resources. Resources has own position or economy has own status, it needs to be at own place. It is the core job of politics to put it at own place and maintain or regulate accordingly, politics job is to ensure highest respect and dignity for human beings or not to make peace, justice, truth, wisdom, dignity etc. as saleable product or cheapest commodity. The wisdom or dignity cannot be defeated or measured by money, truth or justice cannot be defeated or measured by money. To make money for good or welfare is the job of politics, politics for humanity or human victory.

All the conflicts and crises of the world in the history happens for political (nationality or sovereignty) and religious (ideology or religion) reason, few scattered cases may find where exclusively economic resources are main reason in conflict or crises. Conflicts or crises are political and religious luxury, there is no war for poverty. In conflicts and crises economic resources either used as dangerous weapon or it suffered irreparable damages. Instead of protects or preserves and efficient maintenance or proper management human beings creates conflicts and crises in everywhere for their political and religious ambitions. They used resources to destroy the world and nature even, they create nuclear weapon and climate change. The resources highly used against humanity and nature, the world is today highly inhabitable and on the verge of destruction. The development of resources failed to provide peace and prosperity, the misuse and mismanagement of it made the world more complicated and dangerous. Progress comes with challenges, the world has been failed to handle the challenges repeatedly. Economic development is not human development, economic development is inhuman and inhabitable world. The nature is destroying and some artificial resources are creating, the health of world and human beings are not well and safe. What economic development is contributing to the world? Why economic development? Where it is going? Is it for only luxurious conflicts and crises to dehumanize the world? What is the utility of resources?

Resources are being colored, it is no more pure resources but political and religious color is being labeled. It has today ideology or morality and nationality or sovereignty but it does not have humanity and dignity, the resources for submission and conversion. Human beings are the aliens in the world, they do not have any right or freedom on even natural resources of own world. Politicization and theocratization of the resources kills the individual freedom and economic freedom. Politics is war and religion is terrorism, war and terrorism deciding on global resources. It is destroying nature and creating reckless discrimination or oppression, human beings are inhumanely trapped in quick sand. Neither human beings can return to the nature nor artificial systems are giving them any dignified space.

There are resources more than human needs and yet human sufferings are increasing, economic development made the world cruel and complicated only. The deprivation and discrimination is in different forms increasing, poverty and unemployment is recurrent global agenda. Political and religious luxurious propaganda push boundary of human needs high, the rat race and impossible competition has been running in different forms. Political or religious leaders are the manager of the global resources to whom people submit their resources, they gave this world conflicts and crises or made this world a place of hatred and enmity. Resources are no more service in human needs, it became a political and religious competition where human dignity or humanity is completely destroyed. The world has resources more than human needs but it uses for killing humanity, economic policies are being frame for defeating and destroying human. Despite of having enough resources the misuse and mismanagement of it creates extreme crises and human sufferings.

IDEA

Human beings are the son of nature, nature nurture them, and then they kill the nature. Whatever resources the world has today either it is natural or the roots are natural, the start and ends of economy is nature. The world has been took all the possible measures to destroy this nature, all the possible destructive innovation they did to finish it. Human beings are now searching a place out of the world to live, all the resources or economic development failed to save. They lost their roots or home or place of returning, they are fighting to be above nature. Nature is affecting the world, human sufferings are increasing extremely high. Human demands are limitless, nature supplies are limited but more than human needs. The nature has also limitations or ends, misuse and mismanagement of nature is the biggest resources loss or damage. Human beings are not realizing and stop, they are destroying and protecting the nature at the same time. The world is a luxurious buildings that a full of blood and tears, humanless heaven. Nature is the father of economy, understanding and managing the nature properly is real economy. The more understand and manage nature properly, the more efficient and sustainable economy the world will get. Misuse and mismanagement of nature will finish the economy and humanity of the world.

Natural resources means more or less common global resources i.e. air, water, sun, earth, space, oil, minerals, gas, coal (fossil fuels), energy etc., what human did not create but owe. Human beings do not exist or cannot live without natural resources for a moment what they did not create, they can live better without the resources what have they created. Human beings are making efforts to make life easy or better and explore or expand the resources in different forms, they did it by destroying nature and human dignity. Resources has explored and expanded, but it did not make any progress or good for the world and its inhabitants. It causes serious threat to human existence, it makes the world more unsafe and complicated. A dramatic change happens every day as unexpected as mystery, unpredictable conflicts and crises has been increased significantly. Human beings are going beyond the world to space or exploring universe, inequality or discrimination and human sufferings or crises are also going beyond limit parallely. Inhuman and unnatural reckless expansion of the resources are always accidental and destructive, it kills humanity and human existence i.e. nature both.

Equality can be compromised, human dignity can never be compromised. Everyone may not be big, no one is slave or commodity also. Everyone has the inherent right to life and dignity, no one has to be slave or commodity for human basic needs i.e. food, cloth, shelter, education, health etc. It is not only duty and responsibility of state or wealthier but also it is inherent duty of resources itself, everyone has equal right on global resources for his basic human needs. It is not a matter of skill or unskill or employment, it is inherent human rights. It is fundamental duty or responsibility of the politics, it is inherent duty of the resources and human rights on the resources. Anything or any system shall not make potential affect on human dignity, it is human choice but not force or trap.

The exploration and expansion of the resources is great, the blindness or ignorance or corruption is worse. Human systematic slavery or commoditizing human is disaster, suppression or oppression and harmful products or intentional monopoly is crime against humanity. The exploration and expansion of the resources in anyway is serious threat, ignoring the real or relevant conflicts and crises or challenges with expansion is accidental. **Inhuman and unnatural** human efforts for the exploration or expansion of the global resources is the problem, <u>it's a delusional (deception) growth or ballon (gas) growth or hurricane (lantern) growth</u>. It is humanless heaven, footless chair, and inhuman hell. This expansion will explode like ballon with over excess chemical gas or light will be finished like last extreme flash of hurricane lantern before going it's off, suddenly people will discover themselves in a quicksand. This growth or expansion is accidental and suicidal. It enhances deep human's negativity and enmity, all the crime and corruption rise up significantly. It pulls down the human beings in least heinous level where morality and dignity is joke, human became slave and commodity. All the human beings are living in the same world or all the countries are in same planet, human or nature revolts and no one is safe until everyone is. No system works, no one is happy. Only **natural and humane growth** is real growth, it could only give a better world. Truth is not joke, Universal Declaration of Human Rights (1948) is not funny content. Deception with others is first self-deception, you are the first victim of your negativity. Truth is more practice than a piece of paper, paper can never save you or your hypocrisy. UDHR is not novel or literature or poem, it is not a piece of paper. Truth has no connection with documentation, truth has not made of. Truth is truth, truth will be truth. Nothing can change it, documentation cannot make it better or without documentation it never lost. Whatever human beings do is for their own necessity, it may make them better or not. Truth or nature always takes its own course, it never change or lost. Article 1 of UDHR, 1948 is truth, you documented because its truth but documentation does not create it. Document it as mere declaration only but will never consider it in practice to have fun, ignorance and arrogance or asinine makes the whole world dead. Truth is absolute, it has no alternative. It will never spare anyone or anything, everyone has to face truth and pay the highest price. Unequal and undignified extreme growth or expansion is against truth and nature, the destination of this delusional growth is quicksand. If world exists or you alive then economy, otherwise where is market and economy or whose economy or how's economy. <u>Tall is not talent, growth is not great</u>. It is the main function or fundamental responsibility of politics, politics manage the economy or resource management is the main job of politics and politics get the tax or vat or others huge finance with absolute regulating powers for ensuring or maintaining or improving security in every aspects. The security can only be ensured after human rights and human dignity ensured, politics has the enough power and resources to ensure that. Human made the system to work for them is politics, it is the direct public representation. It has enormous power to deal with the issues efficiently, economic failure is political failure.

Corruption (moral, financial, political etc.) and intentional monopoly is killing the economy, decentralization or democratization or socialization of resources and work or service is the savior. Political corruption and resources monopoly is destroying global economy, corruption and monopoly both supports each other on the journey of oppression and human sufferings.

The corrupted politics and monopolize economy is severely wasteful or insensible, harmful or unsustainable and extreme or unstable. It may cause increase some numbers, it decrease human growth or development significantly. This is the dangerous deceptive pandemic of the era, it creates a fix vicious cycle. The corruption never allow economy to be strong, monopoly can never build a sustainable economy. Neither corruption release monopoly nor monopoly can get out of corruption, both destroy the economy together. The idea of state or economy is collective and coordinated, this has born by affirming everyone has the special potentials and right to equal opportunities. All the potential does not owe few people, everyone has the different potential to the best utilize the resources and make a great contribution to the economy. Everyone shall get the share of resources to make efforts to make his potential real, the collective contribution of the individual build great economy. Corruption and monopoly disturb and discourage the people to grow, it stops and pull down the potentials. Corruption and monopoly is the main cause to the highest misuse and mismanagement of global resources. It destroys the renewability and reproductivity of the resources. Climate change is one of the current example of permanent destruction of the global resources, it exploits and killed. It is directly destroy the existence of civilization- natural resources, corruption and monopoly is the murderer of resources either it be natural or human creations which never came back. This kills the nature and life which never came back, it is destined to destroy the world. This creates temporary deception or delusion to cover the crime which is in actual permanent or original or natural or existential destruction. Today the world does not have the resources but some number and papers, the world is today an empty house. This number or papers cannot create or get back the nature and life what they have killed to be a big number, this made irrecoverable damages. Consequently, despite of having resources limited but more than human needs, human beings are suffering today. The deceptive number is increasing but resources are decreasing, few people are enjoying and rest of all other majority is suffering. Corruption and monopoly destroy the resources permanently, whatever resources have is being monopolized and using for deception of number or blaming public incapacity to suppress them. Cutting the trees or selling the kidneys looks became rich for a day, tomorrow is your confirm funeral, enjoy. Corruption and monopoly neither will come to save you nor can save you, they will not save even themselves. No one will be spared, no one will spare no one. No one is safe, neither human nor nature. Corruption and monopoly is unpredictable and serious threat to everything, it destined to destroy anytime. It promotes slavery and commoditize human only, corruption is nothing but oppression and destruction. There is no economy in corruption and monopoly, here is only scam and stupidity. This is not suicide of the economy, this is murder of the economy. This is the real casteism, real racism that gently named inequality or discrimination. Corruption and monopoly is the last weapon to finish the politics and economy both. This is the CAPITALISM, the world needs ETHICAL CAPITALISM.

Occupying more lands is not, proper management of existing resources is true and sustainable victory. Group is more important than growth, connect is more important than increment. Coordination is better than creation, economy is more social than political. Coordinate all the social or economic class or status people and together work or contribute to the society will build a great economy. The development that reach to the last man or unit of the society, connect or coordinate and bring them up or forward to break the cycle to enter into mainstream. When development reach to the last man of the society or every class of the country, it may be more or less but it contributes or improves a bit is development. The development that inclusive but not exclusive, it concerns for every citizen of the country of all levels or classes or categories. The economy where everyone has the participation more or less, no one has deprived or discriminated or excluded. The collective economic participation and the enhanced capabilities to participate of all the stage of society build a great economy. If social backward class is not forwarding or entering into mainstream, there is no economy but scam. Coordination of all social classes or inclusive participation is economy, special concern or support or incentive to bring them up to contribute together is economy. Collective or social or inclusive growth is stable, sustainable and sensible growth. Peace is not mere growth, it is collective obligation. Economy is not number, it's human life.

The way people see the resources or money, the minds behind 1) **demands** and 2) **consumption** has much contributed to the economy. Necessity (natural needs) and luxury (artificial demands) are decided under the political (reason) and religious (system) influences. They cannot consume what they demand, they want security and dignity. People could not use or consume what they demand, they want freedom and capability. When human became actual free, he became more disciplined. Human revolts against force, human became satisfied with one but never stop to take another or change. It varies according to human instinct, someone extreme or quantity matters and someone stable or quality matters.

Expenditure or consumption management is equally important to income or production process management for a better and sustainable economy. Otherwise, limitless resources or income will even make you poor, mismanagement or inefficient management of expenditure will never make you rich or better economy. How to earn or income or produce and how to use or consume or expend are both equally important for a great economy. Resources are trust or makes you custodian, it is a fundamental duty and responsibility to the individual to state all to make its best utilization. Whatever resources anyone does have, it may be more than his needs but it is limited or it has end. The lifestyle or how you live or maintain your life or philosophy of life of individual and state is important to manage expenditure, neither be so parsimonious nor be so extravagant but manages the resources in a moderate or balanced or equitable or just manner where it needs or necessity. Resources shall not be discriminatory or monopolize, the use of it shall not be harmful or accidental for own and others. The sensible and responsible or necessary use or expend of resources ensure sustainable economic growth, resources shall not control human beings in rich or in poverty but human beings shall control and manages the resources. Human beings shall not be trapped and dictated or affected by the resources, human beings shall manage and treat the resources in such a manner so that they shall never surrender or submit before it and not to be slave or blind of it. It is powerful, so be careful. Be ready for any situation, hard work or make constant efforts unstoppable. There is no guarantee of anything in the world, one thing shall never be compromised even before death is dignity. The self-control and control of everything of the world includes economy shall be under human beings, do not lose or compromise self-control and it is daily fight of the life. All the world systems are made for the service of mankind, if any system became bigger than human beings to control them then it definitely would be Frankenstein to make disaster. Resources shall not control you in anyway high or low, it is accidental and suicidal or destructive. So, the income and expenditure or manage the resources sensibly or neutrally and responsibly or necessarily. Discipline is must everywhere. Planned or secured and efficient management of the resources with long term vision and dignity is the road to great economy. Do not ever be emotional with resources in poverty or rich that burnt you to be dust; it is real or practical and intelligent minds business. No waste, no harm, no extremism or excess but sensible, stable or moderate and sustainable management or **treatment** of the resources is the ultimate road to great economy. It has limit, it has an end. So, be safe, utilize it in the best way...

Resource management is fostering or rearing a child, production to consumption or born to death the process is relevant. Necessity or luxury produces the product, it requires material and immaterial raw materials and process i.e. vision, plan, process, labor and capital, design and experiment, safety and quality check, activate and produce, marketing and distribution, free market, transaction i.e. sale and branding, growth, profit, maintenance and upgrade, legacy or brand i.e. build structure or sustainable system, create employment and contribute for the humanity etc. It is secured or planned investment, though there is always calculative risk. No waste, no harm, no extremism or excess but sensible, stable or moderate and sustainable management or **treatment** of the resources is the ultimate road to success. Strong focus on long term vision and creativity or innovation drives the human being, he fights for security and dignity. While there is hope, there is life.

Economic development through ages-

- Construction (land)
- Transportation (water)
- Communication (air/technology)
- Industry (land/processed)
- Science (sky/space)
- Free market
- Imagination (human intelligence)

Expenditures or demands and consumption in priority for a child and state as follows:

1. Food security
2. Education and research
3. National and international security includes judiciary and military
4. Health
5. Infrastructures
6. Transport
7. Labor and employment
8. Market i.e. commerce and industry
9. Finance
10. Science and technology
11. Environment
12. CIVIL SERVANT or GOVERNMENT
13. Reserve fund
14. History, culture and religion

15. Tourism and hospitality
16. Social security or welfare

Income or resources and supply with economic principles:

- Vision and plan with political commitments
- GREAT CIVIL SERVANT i.e. collector
- Natural resources i.e. air, water, sun, earth, space, oil, minerals, gas, coal (fossil fuels), energy etc.
- Resource specialization (reserve and export)
- Agriculture and small businesses
- Self-reliance (self-respect)
- Decentralization or localization
- NGO and CSR programs or funds managements
- Interests free (usury)
- *Haram* products or service free i.e. no alcohol or drugs or gambling or prostitution or tobacco or corruption etc.
- Trained and skilled workforce
- Public or government businesses
- Foreign investments or industries
- Technology (artificial intelligence, space exploration etc.)
- Reserve fund and loan
- Services
- Open and safe market

Mixed economy i.e. free market but government may control if necessary (political economy or economics)

Risk factors are as follows (unpredictable challenges):

- Natural disaster
- Political instability

- Global impact
- Corruption and crime
- Discrimination and inequality or injustice
- Syndicate or monopoly
- Inefficient bureaucracy
- Unskilled workforce or labor issues
- Transportation and communication
- Advanced infrastructures and modern facilities
- Global standard market or global network
- Trust deficit
- Rigid, unplanned and extreme economic policies
- Unsafe situation or environment etc.

Life decides economy or economy decides lifestyle, economy follows the life and life follows the economy. The goal is to build economy in accordance with life, the reality is economy decides the life. Human can control economy, economy controls human beings. Human beings can build a sustainable economy that follow human life, human beings can be suppressed under economy also. Human beings became slave or ruled by economy in the race of winning it, some cases human beings changed in the race of changing economy. Economy is life for someone, for someone economy is death. Poverty is suppressing someone, big economy is pressurizing or disturbing someone. Poverty and wealthy both are destroying life, success destroys the life more than failures. The coordination or balance between economy or resources and dignity or happiness is absent. Either it became so big to worship it or so small to suffer, it is uncontrolled or undisciplined or unorganized or unstructured and unpredictable. Someone is dying in failing to accomplish it, someone is submitting or surrendering to accomplish it. The 1) **sustainability** (resources), 2) **stability** (political) and 3) **sensibility** (cultural) or depthness or quietness in serving mankind is great economy. Human beings are significantly and recurrently failing to manage the resources, failing to absorb or hold this slippery thing and <u>so there is no economy but efforts</u>.

Economy to facilitate human to be individual and independent, he shall not be burden for state. His contributions to the state make it more strong or efficient and more developed or powerful, state ensures the highest respect and dignity for its citizen to the whole world. The systems and institutions has been created for facilitating human beings to be individual and independent, state managed collective contribution to establish and maintain peace and security.

Political influence on economy is decisive, economic policies are important factors in election. Economy is independent and global, politics is dependent and limited. Political corruption or instability or inefficient government destroy the economy, political efficient coordination or management or administration builds big in economy. The main function of political government is resources coordination and resource management, economy is the inherent priority of government. Politics regulate production and consumption or born and destiny of resources, the political power can create big and set the standard or values in serving to the mankind. Economic power is independent and boundless, politics born to set the limit of it to human welfare. Economy gave birth politics, economy can rule the world with politics or without politics. Economy is the biggest and real politics, economy is existential elements to the world. Without economy there is no politics, without politics there is economy. To regulate the economy there needs extraordinary politics, economy eat out the weak politics. Today set the politics through observing economy, the better you handle economy the brighter your politics. Politics can support and guide the economy in a better way, it can make the economy big and sustainable. Can the politics really regulate the economy?

If economy takes out from politics, politics became just few scattered seasonal words. Politics has two main founding pillars- education and economy, without economy it became an ineffective education or NGO or policy research institute which has no power to implement or public recognition. Politics are legal and collective power, it is the job of genius minds or leaders. Politics has the ability to regulate and lead the economy, political mind can control or manage economy efficiently. Without politics resources can be wastage or damage, the anarchist world would begin where economy became valueless but politics will rule. Economy is powerful in the civilized world, the civilized world made and managed by the politics. Politics cultivate the plants in desert or fertile the desert land or manage sweet water in desert, economy just enjoy or be settled here. Politics do sleepless night duty as security guard, economy sleeps to have fun in day. Politics run and serve or save this world, economy live and work here for live. The civilization has been built by blood, not by money. Politics is the market, economy is resources. Politics is human and economy is earth, politics is life and economy is one necessary part of life. Without politics or human the economy or earth became humanless heaven or inhuman hell, economy will be the debris or rubble of Hiroshima- Nagasaki. At the end of the day above all humanity is the existence of the world, not money but economy is one of the important world programs. Analyzing the politics and economy as separate or independent system, under politics economy can be better but as both independent system politics is more powerful than economy. Therefore, politics manages the resources, regulate the economy.

ETHICAL CAPITALISM i.e. individual freedom or free market under government regulations, ethical capitalism is welfarism towards equitable or dignified living. Ethical capitalism is mixed economy, free market under government control. Ethical capitalism is human centric economy or just economy, economy for human welfare and human dignity. The economy will work independently in free market to create wealth and manage resources efficiently to maintain higher growth, politics will drives it to the human welfare and human dignity. A good economy, humanized economy, and quality economy. Business or trade with ethics and values, ethics and values in all the phases of economy like raw materials, production or manufacture, distribution, use or consumption, business or trade, market, profit, transactions or currency etc. Anything shall stop which cause or support injustice or corruption or dehumanization or deprivation or discrimination or harmful to the humanity. Truth, justice and dignity are the constitution or religion of economy, economy is the active forces to enhance and maintain truth, justice and dignity. Ethical capitalism is religious economy, it is the state obligation to regulate strictly. Ethical capitalism is systematic economy but not anarchy, through the necessary policies and measures in time to time politics or state ensure and maintain economy by the truth, justice and dignity. It is an economic culture, economic religion and economic sense. The ethics in capitalism is legally enforceable and politically actionable, capitalism is economy and ethics is politics. Ethical capitalism is political economy, capitalism for good. Politically driven individual freedom or free market economy towards truth, justice and dignity.

Progress and challenges or high and low move on parallaly, good and bad both are world together which will never be stop and one. Conflicts or crises is and will be always there in the world, opportunities or facilities needs to be available and accessible to minimize the problems and maximize the possibilities. Challenges are not barriers but concern and creations of better way to solve it, create more universal space and access to get the more contribution. Crisis is not something to ignore or stoppage or forgotten element, it is concerning and part of the journey. Challenge comes with progress, both needs to be addressed in a possible or proper manner. The world has come through the ages with crises and conflicts, it progressed and addressed the issues in a possible manner. It did neither stop nor ignore. The world will move on or progress, problems will be there that both the world and problem shall make better progress together. Conflicts and crises are never ending concern of the world, progress and possibilities also never ending part of the world. Resolving conflicts is the progress, combat with new crises is the journey. To make utmost efforts to solve, but it shall not stop the journey.

INSTANCE

WORLD ECONOMY POLICY, 2024

Preamble:

> *"The world has limited resources but more than human needs."*

1. Definition (s):

a. There are three familiar terms monetary (individual i.e. money), finance (institution or organization i.e. monetary activity), economy (state or world i.e. policy and management).

b. Economy is not money but resources, money is one converted exchange form of resources only and finance is monetary activity.

c. Everything of this world can be economic resources, resources are driving forces or fuel of this world and service or needs of mankind.

d. Resource is not economy, economy is resource management.

e. Economy is the complete study of resources, the whole life of resource born to death and its great or efficient management is the economy.

f. The external and internal all the relevant factors to the resources are the subject matter of the economy, economy is the blueprint for world future.

2. Vision:

Economy to facilitate human to be individual and independent, he shall not be burden for state.

3. Mission:

ECONOMY (management or political economy) *of* NATURE (resources or economics) and DIGNITY (human or politics)

4. Principle (s):

a. Natural and dignified economy

b. Ethical capitalism i.e. politically driven individual freedom or free market economy towards truth, justice and dignity.

5. Demand (s):

a. Security, and
b. Dignity

6. Management:

a. No waste,
b. No harm,
c. No extremism or excess but
d. Sensible,
e. Stable or moderate and
f. Sustainable management or treatment of the resources is the ultimate road to great economy.

7. System:

a. Sustainability (resources),
b. Stability (political) and
c. Sensibility (cultural) or depthness or quietness in serving mankind is great economy.

8. Policies:

a. Vision and plan with political commitments
b. GREAT CIVIL SERVANT i.e. collector
c. Natural resources i.e. air, water, sun, earth, space, oil, minerals, gas, coal (fossil fuels), energy etc.
d. Resource specialization (reserve and export)
e. Agriculture and small businesses
f. Self-reliance (self-respect)
g. Decentralization or localization
h. NGO and CSR programs or funds managements

a. Interests free (usury)
j. *Haram* products or service free i.e. no alcohol or drugs or gambling or prostitution or tobacco or corruption etc.